11-09

11-09

SHEDDING LIGHT ON MY FAITH
AND MENTAL HEALTH JOURNEY

TODD C. BYMOEN

Print ISBN: 978-1-4866-2305-1
eBook ISBN: 978-1-4866-2306-8

Word Alive Press
119 De Baets Street, Winnipeg, MB R2J 3R9
www.wordalivepress.ca

WORD ALIVE
—P R E S S—

Cataloguing in Publication may be obtained through Library and Archives Canada

To everyone who suffers with their mental health.

CONTENTS

ACKNOWLEDGEMENTS

I'd like to thank my wife, Mandi, everyone in my writing school at YWAM, and also those who have helped me with writing this book along the way.

TWENTY-TWO YEARS OLD

CHAPTER ONE

Hitting the snooze bar for the third time, foggy memories from the night before come to mind. My mouth feels dry and tacky from all the booze and cigarettes, and I long for a glass of water. Pieces of the night entertain my mind as I roll out of my bed. I wander down the hall of my trailer, miles out in the wilderness, forty-five minutes from town, at Crooked Lake camp where I work operating gas wells, compressors, and gas plants. Finally making it to the bathroom mirror, I see an image of a broken, hurting man—maybe just a boy really. I slap some cold water on my face, wanting to go back to bed, not feeling up for the day ahead.

Over a cup of coffee, I reflect on what happened the night before. It's just like the last couple of years; the parties all blend together. The sleepless nights, due to drinking and drugs, compounded with long days at work, are starting to take their toll on me.

I manage to pull myself together and into my company truck, not knowing what the day has for me. The road from Crooked Lake to the Bigstone Road is curvy and narrow, rough and pounded out, full of ruts and potholes. I have about half an hour before I reach my destination. As I bang down the road in my truck, I begin to feel angry and depressed, thinking of how much of a mess my life is: the booze, women, and parties aren't doing it for me. I weep, feeling empty, and tears run down my face, dripping onto my blue coveralls.

Finally reaching my destination at the 11-09 compressor station, about twenty-five minutes southwest of Fox Creek, Alberta, I wail and scream out loud. I punch the dash and steering wheel. But then, I hear it: a still, small voice telling me to pray. I don't hesitate. I open the door of my truck and fall to the ground near an old abandoned wellhead. The day is gloomy and the sky is dark grey. The only thing I can hear was the humming of the compressors. There I am on my knees with my face in the dirt, tears falling to the ground, pounding my fists on the earth. I want to die, and I scream to God, begging Him to save me. All of a sudden, I feel waves of energy rolling through my body and I'm overcome by an amazing peace. It feels as if someone has picked me up off the ground, and I'm floating.

I stop crying and I feel an intense heat on my back; I straighten up and look at the dark grey sky. At that moment, I'm engulfed in the brightest light. All I can think about is Jesus. The light disappears and I stand up; I start to dance and shout out praises to God. At the top of my lungs I yell, "You're real! You're real! I can't believe You're real!"

YOUNGER YEARS

CHAPTER TWO

My parents were the young ages of eighteen and nineteen when I was born. Times were tough in the '80s. My dad worked away from home on the drilling rigs for two weeks at a time. When he was home, he was busy starting a farm from the ground up to provide financial stability for our family. My mom stayed at home for most of my childhood, and then later owned a grocery store in Simmie during my teen years. Both of my parents were hard workers and put their all into providing for us.

My sister and I went to a small school of about thirty kids. There were two rooms—a kindergarten classroom and a larger classroom, which was divided by a library wall. Grades one to three met on one side of the library wall and grades four six met on the other. Every morning, we would line up together as a school to sing "O Canada" and say the Lord's Prayer while our teacher played the piano. School was a place I felt comfortable and secure.

Ever since I can remember, we went to church. My mom would take my sister and me every Sunday. I didn't like church at all because I thought it was boring, and I wasn't sure why I had to go. However, when I was about fourteen years old, I was confirmed and baptized in front of the congregation.

Our farm was only three miles from town, so when we were a bit older, we could ride our bikes to school. Life was pretty simple, and we had a lot of fun growing up this way. After school, I would do my chores, like collecting eggs and maintaining the chicken coop, and then go out to hunt gophers.

After grade six, we were bused to another town for school. So, for grades seven to twelve, I attended Shaunavon Public School. I went from having three classmates in grade six to twenty classmates in grade seven. It was a shock to the system for me. This is when I started struggling with social anxiety. I learned I was insecure and became embarrassed easily. I was full of anxiety most days and lacked confidence. My classmates teased me because I wore cheaper jeans that were too tight, rather than expensive jeans like the cool kids. I was so sensitive that, even if my teacher simply called my name in class, my face would turn bright red. But, despite all of this, during the next five years that I was in high school, I started to become a social butterfly. I started to change a lot through high school. I had been playing hockey since I was four years old, so I excelled at the sport and, therefore, became quite popular. I was friends with most everyone in school. Once, I was asked by the jocks to fight the skaters because they didn't get along. However, I refused, because I was friends with both groups of kids.

When I was sixteen, I got my driver's license. Because I lived fifty miles from where I went to school and played hockey, prior to getting my license, I couldn't do much partying. But, once I got my license, I had more freedom and started to get into the party scene. I became wild when I drank, and often drank too much. When I drank, I didn't feel anxious, and so I learned to be a party animal to hide my anxiety and enjoy the attention I was getting.

Growing up, my sister and I spent a lot of time together talking about life. Once, when I was fourteen, we put our sleeping bags in the back of my dad's truck and slept under the stars. We were pretty good friends most of the time. But like most siblings, we also fought. She was tough, but I still tried my best to be protective of her. However, she could also fend for herself. I remember going to school with a black eye once because I had been teasing her and she decided to fight back.

When I was in grade eleven, my parents divorced after seventeen years of marriage. It was a horrible process and I was a mess, thinking that it was my fault they had a bad relationship. All the pain came to the forefront one day in math class. My teacher was pressuring me about something, and I broke down crying at my desk in the middle of class. My classmates and teacher came around me to console me and helped me to calm down. After I settled down and went for a walk, school was over and I went home. It was a long ride home, since we had to ride the bus one hour each way to school. Obsessive thoughts crowded my mind. Once I arrived home, I broke down again. As I sat in my room crying, I became filled with rage: this was it, I was done. I went to the corner of the porch, where I kept my rifle. I got some shells out of the drawer by the kitchen sink. And then I sat down at the kitchen table and loaded the gun. I pressed the barrel against the temple of my head and was about to pull the trigger. But, at that moment, I thought of my sister. I knew I couldn't leave her alone, so I put the gun away.

A year later, I graduated from high school. Two days after graduation, I moved twelve hours away from home to Fox Creek, Alberta. I wanted to live and work there, because my uncles had done very well in the oil and gas industry. I got a job working as a summer student at an oil and gas company, and I did so well my boss wanted me to stay on to train as an operator. However, because one of my uncles worked there, I wasn't able to get the position. So, I found another job working in construction for a couple months. Then, I received a call from a different gas company, asking for an interview. Two weeks later, I got a job operating gas wells and compressor stations. I worked ten hours a day for eight days straight, and then had six days off. I hit the jackpot financially and was doing really well for myself. At eighteen years old, I was making about $45,000 dollars a year. But, during this time I was also becoming more addicted to alcohol and drugs.

LOST

CHAPTER THREE

Crawling around on the floor, as my friend and his wife laughed feverishly, I felt the burn in my lungs from holding in the crack cocaine I had just inhaled. My friend's children were downstairs, and I had just said "hello" to them as I climbed the stairs to get high with my friend and his wife. However, the high was short lived.

The two times I got high on crack weren't enough to entice me to continue. Instead, I felt shame and guilt each time. When I was at their house, I felt the depravity of what we were doing with innocent children just downstairs, so I ended up going back for the last time and gave the kids all my video game equipment. To me, it was a way of giving something valuable that would mean a lot, since their parents had taken so much from them to feed their addiction.

I lived in Fox Creek for about a year and met some great people there. Then, I ended up moving to Edmonton for about a year, but still remained in the same job. Since I worked in a camp, I could live anywhere I wanted when I wasn't on duty. I moved into a townhouse with a couple buddies and partied a lot. I took a year off hockey and turned to playing video games and smoking weed for my entertainment. My lack of exercise showed, and I gained twenty pounds that winter.

When I was twenty, I started to miss small town life. I had an opportunity to move to Valleyview, Alberta, which was a small town, so I took it. I had become best friends with a coworker, a guy named John, who lived in Valleyview. I found a place to stay with a family friend. Valleyview had a senior hockey team, so I started playing hockey again, and was able to get to know a lot of people quickly. It was a rough and tumble, small Western town, and I loved it because it reminded me of home. I continued with my lifestyle of drugs, alcohol, and women. I was even smoking dope at work every once in a while at this point. Sometimes, I would go straight from partying to work the next morning—drunk. I was always looking forward to the weekend and the next drink. I was reckless and had no direction.

By the time I was twenty-two, many of my relationships were characterized by fighting, and it was wearing on me. I was stressed out most of the time, but never really dealt with anything. It seemed better to just continue pushing all my emotions further down inside of me. I tried to be strong and put up a good front. But, I was insecure about myself and often anxious. I longed for a sense of security.

BACK TO TWENTY-TWO

CHAPTER FOUR

Not long after I had my supernatural experience with God, I began to feel very alive. It was extreme, to the point that I was getting very little sleep, because my mind would race with grandiose and delusional thoughts. I was coming up with so many bogus ideas and acting on them. I remember driving down the road on my way to my best friend John's house, while thoughts blurred in my mind. After rolling into the driveway of his house, I nervously walked to the door. John's girlfriend answered the door, probably confused, but she welcomed me with a smile and told me to come in. While sitting at the kitchen table, I told her that I thought she should be in a relationship with me and not John. I also went on to tell her that I thought it would be a good idea for John to be with someone else I knew. As I was saying this, I saw the fear and confusion in her eyes. I knew it was time to go. My relationship with John wasn't the same after that.

That same day, a different friend called me, and asked if I wanted to go partying in Grande Prairie. I was feeling great, so I said "yes," and we went. The first thing we did was go to an exotic dance club for drinks. One of the dancers kept coming over to talk to us, and we became friends with her that night.

Later that night, while at different bar, I saw the same woman talking to my friend across the room, so I went over to them and started chatting. I realized right away that she looked stressed, so I asked her what was wrong. She told me to look over my shoulder. When I did, I saw two greasy-looking dudes in worn-out black leather jackets. I turned to her and told her that we would get her out of there safely and take her to her hotel room.

At her hotel room, my friend decided to sleep on the extra bed, but I stayed awake and sat with the woman, talking. She asked me if I wanted to do some cocaine and I said "yes." Snort after snort, I inhaled the white powder up my nose, while she did the same. Even though I was influenced by the drugs, I had enough coherence to tell her about my life and my recent experience with Jesus. I ended up preaching to her for a long time until she fell asleep. Then, I got up, woke up my buddy, and we left.

Back at my apartment, I tried to sleep, but my mind was racing. I felt convicted about things I had done and continued to do. So, I decided to dump all of the alcohol from my fridge down the drain.

A day or so later, I started looking through an auto-trader book at my apartment and found my dream truck, one I had always wanted to own: an old 72 Chevy GMC with three blue pinstripes down the side. And, it was for sale in St. Paul, Alberta. The next day I got a call from my mom, who lived in Saskatchewan. I told her that I was heading to St. Paul to pick up my new truck. At this point I hadn't slept for about three days, and the cocaine probably wasn't helping matters. My mom said she was on her way up to see me, so I thought she could give me a ride to get my new wheels.

It was a cold night as I brought the truck back to my aunt and uncle's house in Fox Creek. I was having so much fun and felt like a little kid with my new truck. But, as my mom and I went into the house and greeted my family, they sat me down at the kitchen table and told me that I was sick and needed to go to the hospital. I refused and told them I had never felt this good in my life; why would I go to the hospital? They were persistent and told me that if I didn't go to the hospital, they would have the police come to escort me. I agreed to go.

When we arrived at the hospital, I was taken into a room. A doctor came in and sat down in front of me across the table. He was kind and told me that I was manic and that I needed to go to Grande Prairie, which had a hospital with a mental health ward. I argued with him, but eventually gave in. They took me by ambulance all the way to the hospital. It was weird for me to be strapped down in an ambulance, and yet, I was strangely joyful. I even had a great conversation with the attendant during the entire trip there. I arrived in two hours and realized that they had taken me by ambulance for my safety and others'. As soon as we arrived, I was escorted into a small, blue, padded room, where I had to wait for a short time while they got my room ready.

I wasn't scared at all during this time, but instead felt excited, even though I should have been exhausted. As I look back on these events, some parts are a little blurry. I remember that I was given my room and had to settle in. I had never been inside the mental health ward before and met new people right away—both nurses and patients. Everyone was friendly and hospitable. I started to get to know the other patients and spent time telling them about Jesus. A male nurse told me to come and have a meeting with him. He told me I was manic and wanted me to take two little blue pills. I argued with him, but he told me that I could either take them on my own, or they would have to strap me down and force me to take them. I didn't like the idea of that, so I took the pills right away. It wasn't long before I was asleep in bed from the pills, as they made me very tired.

I woke up the next morning and found out that I had been asleep for fifteen hours straight. Although I had all that sleep, I was still "flying high" mentally. I continued to meet people in the hospital and constantly brought up Jesus in conversations. I even started a small Bible study group with six other patients. Because I was still so new to this Christian life, I didn't know much of the Bible myself, but I knew that Jesus had come to earth, died for my sins and the sins of others, and that whoever believed in him would have eternal life. Looking back, it was probably more of a group for moral support because we were all in the mental health ward together. I can recall writing messages of encouragement on the white boards in the hospital, because I was so happy and full of love for people. I had a burning desire to help others.

A week later, a pastor from one of the local churches came to visit our group. All I can remember is that I shared a lot about what I had experienced when I met Jesus during my low point in life. We also listened to the pastor's message. He answered some of our questions and then it was over. As we walked out of the room, the pastor called to me, grabbed my hand with both of his, and said that he would never forget me. I'll never forget the look on his face—a face full of joy with tear-filled eyes.

Another week went by before I had a meeting with the doctor. That day was the first time I heard the words "Bipolar disorder." I really didn't like those words and thought to myself, "There's nothing wrong with me." I was confused by what the doctor was talking about. He recommended that I stay for a while longer, and he put me on medication. I learned during this time that Bipolar 1 is a mood disorder, which is characterized by lengths of racing thoughts, ideas, psychosis, little sleep, and heightened confidence. Often, when coming down from a high, you can fall into a deep depression. Moods can last from weeks to months at a time if not treated. Triggers can be loss of sleep, high stress, and failure to take medication.

I had been in the hospital for two weeks by this time, and everything seemed fine until I left. Then reality hit me like a brick. People would know about how I had been acting and possibly about the new diagnosis. The worst part was that I had to go back to work and face everyone. This is when I fell into a depression—something I was warned about in the hospital. I felt exhausted and stressed out, but still had to continue on with life. I ended up going back to work, but was so embarrassed to show my face anywhere I went. It was horrible to wonder what people thought of me. However, I pushed forward and tried to ignore what had happened. I felt like everyone thought I was loony and crazy, so I stopped talking about God as well and just brushed my faith under the rug.

GOING OFF THE RAILS AGAIN

CHAPTER FIVE

After I left the hospital, I moved back to Fox Creek and continued to live an unhealthy, immoral lifestyle. I didn't take my doctor's advice seriously, and I ignored my medications and diagnosis. Even my new-found relationship with Jesus wasn't changing how I lived my life. I still struggled and kept going back to my addictions to comfort me. Drinking and smoking weed was just a normal part of my life. I was on a downward slope, making a lot of bad choices. I was still so embarrassed about being put in a hospital.

By the time I was twenty-six years old, I was working as a gas plant operator on the Bigstone Road, putting in a ton of overtime and getting pretty stressed out. At the same time, I was in a terrible romantic relationship in which all we did was fight.

Eventually, a man I called Coach came to work as our plant lead, and we became good friends because we had a lot in common. I often told him about the details of my life and the kind of lifestyle I was living. One day, he stopped me suddenly and asked me how I could be living the way I was if I truly believed in Jesus. I was really caught off guard by his comment. It made me think about my life more.

As time went on, Coach and I became even better friends. After my girlfriend and I broke up, he noticed that I wasn't doing so well with work and the breakup. Around that same time, he had decided to quit his job with the company and move closer to his family near Camrose, Alberta. He also said that he was going to coach a junior hockey team there. As we were talking about these changes in his life, he suggested I come help him coach the team and find a new job. He said it seemed like I could use a change in my life. So I thought about it and decided it was a really great idea. After he left, I put in my resignation at work. All of a sudden, everything started to fall into place. I sold my house right away in a private deal and found a new job just outside of Camrose at the local Cargill Grain Terminal, as well as a basement bedroom for rent.

One night, I was over at Coach's house for supper, talking over plans for the Junior B hockey tryouts, when he gave me my first Bible. I went home and started reading it right away. I was starting to feel like a new man who had been in prison for a long time and was finally set free. I was beginning to know my worth for the first time in my life, which brought me so much happiness.

My new job was awesome. I had set hours and worked with some really great people. Things were changing for me. At times it seemed too good to be true.

Hockey started up. Coach and I would travel—sometimes together, sometimes separately—to Killam, Alberta, for practices and games. I was so excited about coaching, though not fully thinking through my decisions at that time, that I even went out and bought $700 worth of dress clothes so I would look sharp on the bench as an assistant coach.

During the times that I drove myself to Killam for hockey, I would drive past a certain road that made me curious about what was down it. I had a feeling about this road each time I passed it, and I later realized that God was nudging me to drive down it. So, one day, I decided to follow my hunch. I came to a farm with lots of trees around it. At that time, the gate at the entrance to the yard was closed, so I turned around and went home. One week later, as I was driving that way, I again felt as if something kept telling me I should go back to that farm. So I did. This time, the gate was open. I drove in and parked in the middle of the yard. It was early fall and there were birds every-where. I hollered out loud to see if anyone was home. An old woman came out of the garden, and an old man came out of the barn. They asked me why I had come to their place, and I told them I believed God must have told me to, because I felt led to come here for some reason. They just smiled and said they wanted to show me something. So, I followed them to a little trailer on their property. When I looked inside, I saw a Bible, scripture verses on the walls, and a guest book in which to sign my name. They said that it was a prayer trailer used for evangelism. I had a really great visit with them and was so encouraged by our conversation. Before I left, they both took my hands and prayed for me. I was so excited by what had happened to me. It caused me to wonder about God more and how He might choose to speak to me.

I was having a good time coaching hockey, I had started dating the woman whose house I was living in, and I had a great job. However, in the midst of all of the positive changes in my life, I still wasn't getting enough sleep, which I would later find out is a trigger for mania for those with Bipolar disorder. I started to argue with Coach about how he was leading our hockey team. Thoughts rolled through my mind at high speeds, and I started to do some weird things. I even called Coach in the middle of the night and asked for money. I was acting very strange.

During that time, the thought came to mind that I needed to see my sister. So, I jumped in my car in the middle of the night and drove five hours to Hinton, Alberta. I showed up in the morning and was greeted by my sister's roommate. My sister wasn't even at home and was supposed to be gone for a couple days. I had forgotten that. I was manic at the time, but didn't know it myself.

On the way home, I felt wired and full of emotion. I was also driving too fast, and a police officer pulled me over for speeding. When he came to my window, I was in a full-blown meltdown, crying uncontrollably. He still gave me a ticket.

As I continued on towards home, I got a call from my mom asking me to stop at my aunt and uncle's house in Beaumont, Alberta. On my way there, I met up with a friend, who I knew through my family, who invited me to get together for supper. I didn't know at the time, but learned later that my family asked him to meet me for supper so he could assure that I arrived safely at my aunt's house. My family was very concerned about my mental health.

When I got to my aunt's house, I was greeted by even more of my family, not just my mom. I spent the night there and, the next day, my family confronted me. They told me that I needed to go to the hospital, but I resisted. In my manic state, I thought everyone was going crazy. I started preaching about Jesus to them. Looking back, I realize that I was being forceful in my approach and not very loving because of the mania. I was saying everything on my mind. I even got into a yelling match with my uncle on the lawn. He shared his concern and told me that I was manic, but I continued to insist that I wasn't. In the end, my family called the police to take me to the hospital.

It's interesting to me that even during the times when my mental health was at its worst, God still used some of the words out of my mouth. Though I was struggling, I also had a boldness to share about Jesus in the midst of not being mentally sound—a boldness that has often been even more evident than when my mental health is good. During the times of mania, my spiritual passion for evangelism is heightened. I lose my fear of people, embarrassment, or self-consciousness. So, while negative events have definitely taken place during my manic episodes, I also know that God has used me because of my boldness.

Once again, I was back in the hospital in the mental health ward. This time, a security guard sat by my door twenty-four-seven to monitor me for the first week. I hadn't even been in Camrose for a month and there I was, in the hospital. I was still on a manic high for about my first two weeks in the hospital, and then I crashed. This time, my doctors kept me at the hospital longer in order to monitor me. After three weeks there, I finally came to terms with my illness. This was the beginning of a long journey of accepting the reality that I had Bipolar disorder. Sadly, somewhere in the mix of being in the hospital and trying to get better, my life drastically fell apart. I had to quit my job, my girlfriend ended our relationship, and I had to step down from the hockey team. I was depressed and embarrassed. I wanted to crawl into a hole and die.

So, here I was at rock bottom again. After being discharged from the hospital, I found myself at my uncle's house in Beaumont again. I was confused about life and didn't know what was going to happen because of my mental illness. But, this time, I knew to pray about it. Then out of the blue, an old friend I hadn't talked to in years called me. We chatted about life and he said that he and his brothers were moving home to run the family farm. He mentioned playing some hockey with a hometown team in the senior league—the Shaunavon Badgers—that winter. After I got off of the phone with him, I decided that this was my next step. I would move to my mom's house in Swift Current, Saskatchewan, and play hockey for the season. So, I talked it over with my mom and stepdad. They said that I could move in with them for the winter so I could get back on my feet.

When I got back home and settled in, I told myself I would try to go to church. One Sunday, I went to the Lutheran church in town by myself. I sat down in the back row and, within ten minutes of being there, my shirt was soaked in sweat. Sweat was also pouring off my head. I was having a really bad anxiety attack. I felt awful inside and thought that everyone was looking at me. I was terrified. I got up and left before the service even started.

Despite this incident, the winter went really well in terms of hockey. I had a lot of fun. We even won our league title that year. The next spring, I got a new job in Shaunavon, Saskatchewan, as an oil operator and moved into a little one bedroom house. The new job went well and life seemed to become somewhat normal again.

AFRICA

CHAPTER SIX

Life in Shaunavon was great. I was so happy to be near home, working in a great job and having money again. I was even a part of the local volunteer fire department. It was interesting though, that after ten years of being in the oil and gas industry, and earning a lot of money, I was still living paycheck to paycheck because of partying. However, my partying had started decreasing because of my experiences with God. I also started to meet more Christians. I saw how they lived and wanted the good things they had in their lives.

I was hungry to know more about God and soon a friend of mine invited me to a Bible study. When I arrived, I was surprised to see about fifteen men hanging out and having a great time. I had never experienced such a thing without alcohol. After the Bible study was over, I went home, knelt by my bed, and prayed that God would change my life and speak to me through His word. After that, the Bible became alive to me. I wanted to know more and more of God's word.

My new friends invited me to church, and I started going with them. I had an anxiety attack every time I entered the church, but I kept going anyway. I just couldn't get enough of what I was learning. Everything started to change for me. Up until that time, even though I was learning what was right, I had continued to live a sinful lifestyle. I had always learned the hard way, because I was rebellious. But, this time, I started to feel convicted of my drinking and sleeping with women outside of marriage. By the time I turned thirty, I quit drinking and smoking. I knew I needed to give up my partying lifestyle. I even stopped hanging around old friends and started to get more involved in church.

During this time, I had started dating a woman from Regina, Saskatchewan. Whenever I had days off, I made the trip to visit her. I also started to attend her church when I could. I loved her church so much; it was so alive. Through her church, I got the opportunity to go on a mission trip to Zambia, Africa. Just before we left to go to Africa, I was baptized in front of the whole church. It was an exciting time in my relationship with the Lord.

I had a beautiful experience in Africa. Our team of fifteen stayed at an orphanage for three weeks. We put on a Vacation Bible School with a whole school of kids for a week and spent another week doing construction projects

for the orphanage. I was so impacted by the children's stories about their home lives. So often they lived without any
food and suffered abuse of all kinds. The school was their
safe place to be each day. They would line up at the gate in
the morning, excited to be there early. Broken and humbled, I cried a lot over those three weeks. Although these
children went through so much, they were always smiling
and happy to see us. I was so thankful that I got to be a part
of the trip.

While on the trip, we often played soccer with the
children. One thing that bugged me, though, was a tree
root sticking out of the ground, right in the middle of the
soccer field. Every time we played, we would have to watch
for it so that we didn't trip while we ran around. One day
while driving into the orphanage, I spotted a pickaxe lying
on the ground. I thought, "These are God's children, and I
want to protect them and bless them."

That evening, I found the pickaxe and started to dig
up the tree root. Little did I know that God would use this
physical work to do spiritual work in me at the same time.
The root turned out to be a big taproot that went deep
into the ground. But, I was determined. As I dug up and
chopped off piece by piece of the root, I was overcome by
emotion because I sensed God speaking to me, that these
pieces of the root represented my past bondage. Just as I

removed each piece, He removed each bondage from my life. I wept and rejoiced every time I chopped off another root. I worked at it for some time until I was called in to eat. I knew I couldn't finish the large task alone, so I asked a friend to come help me after supper. It took a bit of work, but we finally got the root out of the ground. I was so proud of digging up the root, and I was thankful for the way that God had "dug up" the bondage of my life. I had my picture taken with the root as a reminder.

★★★

Unfortunately, the plane ride home was scary for me. I started to become paranoid, and my mind raced as thoughts bombarded me. I actually thought the guy sitting in front of me had a bomb. When we arrived at our layover and waited for the connecting flight, I thought our airport was going to get bombed. I was absolutely terrified. I wouldn't have made it home to Regina without the support of my girlfriend coaching me.

After we returned, I stayed at my girlfriend's house while she worked the next day. That day, I realized I was having another manic episode, during which I wrote down all of the crazy thoughts in my mind, filling page after page. When my girlfriend got home, I told her about things that had been happening to me before and after the trip to Africa. I told her that, earlier that day while she was at work, I was in the bath, when all of a sudden I heard a loud banging noise coming from the pipes, as if someone was in the bathroom with me. I was frozen with fear and couldn't move. The noise went away and I ended up carrying on with my day. I mentioned to her that I had the same experience in my own home prior to the trip. I also told her about the time I played with an Ouija board as a kid. And, I told her that I had seen a ghost once, on the farm when I was growing up.

After telling her all these things, she asked me to pray with her. I agreed. She took my hand and asked me to repeat after her. She spoke against the evil spirits I had been experiencing, and she wanted me to speak out against them as well. But, when I tried, I tensed up. My mouth wouldn't repeat what she said. With all my might, I blurted out what she said, and I felt something leave me. I laid on the couch lifeless—completely out of strength. After that night, I have never been haunted by those evils again.

About two weeks after those events, my girlfriend broke up with me. It really hurt to lose that relationship. However, looking back, I can see the positive things God was teaching me, including how important it was for me to take my medications and take my illness seriously. After coming out of this emotional time, I sold my house and spent a summer wrangling horses and giving riding lessons to kids at a Bible camp. I thought about going to Bible college in the fall, but God had other plans, and I ended up back in Shaunavon doing construction work. During this time, I started helping with the seniors' ministry and youth group at my church, until, eventually, I was leading the youth group. Finally, I bought a nice acreage south of town, where I made so many memories.

STIGMA

CHAPTER SEVEN

I have always enjoyed driving in the prairies—cruising down the road on autopilot, daydreaming about anything. I was on my way to Regina one day and, in my relaxed state, passed by a hitchhiker. I didn't think too much about it at first, but then I kept getting the urge to go back and pick him up. I've always enjoyed picking up hitchhikers. It's always interesting to meet new people and help them out. So, I took the next exit and crossed onto the westbound highway. Heading back the direction I had come, I saw that he was still there. I whipped across at the next approach and drove up to him. He was in winter gear, since it was late fall. Sporting a green, down-filled jacket, black toque, and a backpack with a bright orange flag hanging from it, he walked up to my vehicle. I rolled down the window of my old blue truck and was met with a joyful face and beard to match his bright red cheeks. He introduced himself as Dave, we talked briefly about where he was headed, and he jumped in. It wasn't long into the drive that I found he had a love for Jesus. As I usually do with hitchhikers, I brought up the topic of Jesus, because I have a love for sharing the good news with people. I especially enjoy sharing with hitchhikers, because, really, where can they go? By the time we hit Herbert, a town about half an hour from Swift Current, we were in full blown conversation.

As we talked, I realized that Dave was a highway evangelist. He shared with me that he had hitchhiked across Canada five times, sharing Jesus with all who would hear. He was a jovial character, at times breaking into worship, singing out loud as I drove on towards Regina. During our conversation, he quoted a lot of scripture to me; I was impressed by his knowledge of the Bible and other topics. He asked me about my life story, so I told him about my childhood and where I was from, and how I came to have a relationship with Jesus. I told him about my diagnosis of Bipolar disorder, the times I'd been hospitalized, and the different medications that I'd been on. Dave was listening attentively up until that point, but then interrupted me. He said that if I had better faith, I wouldn't have this disorder and that I shouldn't be on medication. He told me his thoughts about the pharmaceutical business and how it was all about the money that could be made. Don't get me wrong, I do believe some of what he was saying. At the time in my life when I met him, I was also pretty impressionable, and gave some thought to what he was saying. I was still young in the faith and easily swayed.

Before we knew it, we had made it to Regina. I was so intrigued by this man and our conversation that I ended up driving him an extra forty-five minutes past Regina to another town along the highway. While I parked, I felt led to give him some money for his travels. I pulled out $300 in cash and handed it to him. Dave took the money and said that I was very generous. He thumbed through the bills, took out $10, and then gave me back the rest. I looked at him questionably, and he explained that he only took a small amount so that he had to rely on the Lord for his needs. We said our goodbyes and I turned around and headed for Regina.

As I drove back towards the city, I wrestled with what he said about lack of faith and medication. At this point, I had been doing quite well on my new medications and was having some victory in my life with my mental health. But, I was so impacted by Dave, I decided to go off my medication. It wasn't long after that day—weeks, maybe a month—before I ended up going downhill. I remember talking with my girlfriend at the time about the events and she must have told some of my friends, because it wasn't long before they told me I was manic and should see a doctor.

Fortunately, I had a really good doctor at the time who helped me to see the need for medication, and soon I was back to level again. I learned the importance of medication and came to terms with the fact that not all people understand mental health and the stigma around it, even in the Church.

ROCK SOLID

A round this time, my buddy Nolan and I drove out to visit a youth ministry called Rock Solid Refuge, a twelve-month residential program for troubled teenage boys struggling with life-controlling issues, just outside of Shaunavon. I was asked to share my testimony with the boys that night. I had never shared my story with a group before, and I was terrified. But, that night around the bonfire, I shared my life story and how I had come to be a Christian. After I finished, the young guys started coming up to me and sharing their stories too. It was so wonderful to be able to connect with these teenage boys.

About a year later, in 2012, I became a youth care worker at the same ministry. During my time as a youth care worker, I learned so much about myself, others, and God. I learned to love unconditionally and be more like Jesus as I served others.

Teaching teenage boys boundaries and holding them accountable can be very challenging. I loved the boys so much and wanted to be someone that I wish I could've had in my life at their age. Ultimately, I wanted them to see Jesus, to know the love of Jesus, and to know they are loved no matter what they do. It was amazing to see how God was using my past to help me understand these teen-age boys and have empathy for them. Unfortunately, by the time I had worked at Rock Solid Refuge for eighteen months, my mental health started to decline and I went on another manic high.

During the high, I felt like God was telling me to go to Walmart and get a map. So I went and wandered around the store, wondering why I was there looking for a map. Eventually, I found them at the front entrance of the store. While I was standing there, I thought that I really didn't need a map, and I asked God why I was there. Then, I thought that I should start telling people about Jesus. So, I talked with many other customers about Jesus and, after a while, I felt thirsty. I went to the McDonald's in the Walmart and got a drink. While I was sitting down in the middle of the restaurant and talking with a bunch of regu-lars, I noticed a tall stool in the middle of the restaurant. I climbed up on it and yelled out to get everyone's attention. The restaurant became silent. I shared a small testimony about what Jesus had done in my life with the crowd in about thirty seconds. As I got down from the stool, a lot of people clapped. Then, an old lady stood up and came up to me. In a loud voice, she praised God and said that we needed to "hear more of this."

After leaving the McDonald's at Walmart, I went to a casino and handed out gospel tracts. After I was finished, I got in my car to leave. A worker from the casino tapped on my window. He said that I wasn't allowed to come into the casino and hand out that kind of literature. I told him I didn't realize that I wasn't allowed. He said he was a believer too, but it was his job to tell me the rules.

I ended up standing up in three more restaurants that week and sharing a short testimony of what Jesus had done in my life. During that time, I also went on a ski trip with some youth from Rock Solid Refuge and, while in the chalet, felt the same urge to get on a chair and share with the people there. I started preaching about Jesus, but a woman who worked at the chalet told me I had to stop. I sat down quietly, but, at that moment, someone who was encouraged by what I said came over and gave me a $100 bill toward our trip.

I went home that night and prayed about what I should do next. I felt like I should hand out tracts to everyone at the next wing night following my rec hockey game. I was terrified, but I did it!

One of the positive things that the high compelled me to do was read my Bible for several hours each day. One night, I went to Swift Current to see my mom. She asked me how I was doing. Despite the way I was acting, I told her everything was awesome and that she shouldn't worry. I wasn't able to see what was happening in my own life.

The next morning, I was on my way to Shaunavon for church. When I was halfway there, I felt like I should stop at the gas station across the highway for some reason. I told myself "no" because I didn't want to be late for church since I was singing on the worship team that day. But, as I drove, I continued to get this nudge to go back to the gas station. So, I finally relented and drove back. I prayed and asked God why He wanted me to go back. As I entered the gas station, I saw a man standing at the till, looking really stressed. I asked him what was wrong, and he told me his van ran out of gas. I asked him if he needed help and offered my assistance. He gladly accepted, and I gave him a ride down the highway to his van.

During the five minute drive down the highway, I asked him how he was doing and he poured out his heart to me, sharing everything that was going on in his life. We got to his van and put fuel in the gas tank, but it still wouldn't start, as the battery was dead. I pulled my car around and hooked up the booster cables. He tried to start it again, but it wouldn't start. He kept pumping the gas and trying to start the van. I smelled gas, so I figured the engine was flooded. I walked around to the driver's seat and saw that he had his head on the steering wheel, crying. I encouraged him that everything would be okay and asked him if he believed in prayer. He didn't seem convinced, but we bowed our heads and I prayed. He told me that he was in a hurry because he needed to be in Yorkton, Saskatchewan, by a certain time. I said he was going to make it.

I told him to try starting the van again. He did and it fired up immediately with one turn of the key. I was so happy and praised the Lord. I went to my car, brought back a Christian book on spiritual warfare I was reading at the time, and gave it to the man. He thanked me and left. Even though I was going through a manic time, God still was working in the midst of it. Believe it or not, I still made it to church and sang that morning.

I don't know how I managed to go on like this day after day. This manic high lasted for at least a month. It caught up with me one night while attending a party, where four good friends approached me and told me that I wasn't healthy and that I needed to go to the hospital. They explained to me, "Even though you're doing good things, you're becoming arrogant and unhealthy." This was the third time in my life where family or friends came together to get me help. I accepted what they said, and they drove me to the hospital that night. I had to meet up with my doctor the next day so that he could adjust my medications. I didn't stay at the hospital this time, but instead was allowed to stay with family, for a while, to be monitored.

After I came out of the depression that follows a high, I went back to work. At this time, I was still working at Rock Solid Refuge, but I had switched roles to be a maintenance worker.

I spent a few months doing this job. Even though I enjoyed being at the ministry, my role of maintenance worker wasn't good for me because it didn't follow a routine and required me to be alone a lot of the time. There were also problems with my finances. I wasn't making enough money to keep up with the payments on my acreage and my credit card bills were racking up. It wasn't long before I came to my bosses and broke down crying. I admitted I was so stressed out and couldn't continue in the job. I told them that I needed to go to a hospital for help. I really should have done it a month earlier, but my pride got in the way. I was experiencing so much stress that it was affecting my physical body, to the point that I was walking like an old man. My doctor wanted to admit me to the hospital for a month to work with my medications. I didn't think it was a good idea because I knew I needed to work, but my family encouraged me to do this, as it would be beneficial in the long run. It was a hard decision, but I decided to do it.

It was miserable at the hospital. At first, I was angry at God and felt abandoned and alone. Because of my finances, I came to the knowledge that I needed to file for bankruptcy. I cried for days over this realization. I had nowhere else to turn. But, in the end, this made me dig deep and put my trust in God. I am so thankful for my family and friends who walked through this time with me. I eventually came out of depression while in the hospital with the help of the nurses, doctors, friends, and family encouraging me.

YWAM

CHAPTER NINE

In 2016, after my depression, I got a new job at a construction company. I also filed for bankruptcy and moved into town to rent a room from a friend.

During the eight months I worked at a construction company, I started to help out at Rock Solid again, covering a shift here and there for the youth care workers' holidays. I loved it and was eventually offered the opportunity to go back full-time. It was great to work with the boys again. My mental health was good. I had started to take a sleeping medication, which was making a huge difference in my life. It helped me to stop thinking and actually sleep. I was feeling more rested and had a clearer mind. I was also going to the hospital every couple of months for blood work to check my lithium levels.

So here I was working full-time as a youth care worker and feeling level again mentally. It was such a relief to be working and contributing to society once more.

But, after about a year and a half, I started to feel like I should move on and do something different. It was on my heart to go into missions. I began to search for mission trips and thought about going to Bible college. During this period, I was trying online dating. I met a really sweet woman, and we became good friends. I told her about my desire to do missions or go to Bible college, and she told me about Youth With A Mission (YWAM), an organization with which she was involved. Though I had heard of it, I thought it was only for young people coming straight out of school. However, she told me about a program called Crossroads, a Discipleship Training School for people who are thirty years old and older. Though my relationship with that woman didn't last, I began to pray and seek out the Crossroads program. I found one offered in Lakeside, Montana, and applied, thinking "Why not go for it?" I was accepted into the school a month later.

By the fall of 2017, I was starting to get burned out working with the youth. I decided to quit after Christmas, as I felt like my mental health was slipping again into depression. I moved into my mom's house, spent time resting, and got ready to go to YWAM Montana for the Crossroads Discipleship Training School. Though I was worried and scared about doing something outside of my comfort zone, I was also feeling excited about what God was going to do in my life. I didn't know it, but I was entering into a new season of my life. The first day of school happened to be April 2, 2018—the same day as my thirty-eighth birthday!

I celebrated with seventeen new classmates, plus our leaders. That same evening, we shared our life stories, and I was anxious about sharing mine. After we ate the cake, it was my turn. I was so nervous, I cried for most of my time as I told the ups and downs of my life, as well as how God had been there for me, to a group of total strangers. However, God gave me the strength to be vulnerable with the group as I poured out my heart.

Over the next three months, we had classes on many Biblical topics from a new speaker each week. Then, we started preparing for our two-month outreach mission—we were going to Mexico! Our team had the privilege of spending two months working with the staff of the new YWAM base in Puerto Vallarta, Mexico. We spent our time working with the local churches and organized three week-long Vacation Bible Schools for kids from different areas, built a playhouse for an orphanage, and ran a soccer ministry with about thirty-five kids twice a week. We also put on a basketball tournament and spent time with the locals on weekends putting on carnivals for kids. We even helped to clean up a park and did a bunch of painting. I was able to share my testimony a couple times while I was in Mexico: once at a church and once at a prison. God gave me the opportunity to go to a Mexican jail and share my story to a room full of prisoners.

Mexico was amazing, and the five months of training school went by so fast.

MANDI

CHAPTER TEN

During the training school, I had gotten to know a woman named Mandi, who was in my class, and we had become really good friends—so much so that we started dating as soon as school was over.

After we graduated from the training school, Mandi came back to Canada with me for a visit to meet my family. After spending a couple weeks in Canada, we flew to Pennsylvania, and I spent two weeks there visiting her family and friends. But, after I'd been home about a week, I broke it off with Mandi. I wasn't feeling right about our relationship and thought it was for the best.

I moved back into my mom's house after the training school and, a month later, started working at a carpet cleaning job. I was enjoying my time working and was finally able to process the last five months of my life. My time at YWAM was really intense in many good ways. I learned so much that rocked my world, and my faith and relationship with God had grown immensely. It took me a while to reflect and make sense of it all. I did a lot of praying and was trusting God for what was to come next.

After a couple months, Mandi and I started to talk again every once in a while, until we were talking almost every day. I began to wonder what God was up to and felt that something was about to change in the fall of 2019. I wasn't sure what it was, but I knew I wanted to be in ministry of some sort. So, I began to apply to Bible colleges, again thinking about learning the Bible. A few more months of working passed, when I started thinking about something that had been on my heart for a number of years: writing a book. I came to the conclusion that I wanted to try writing a book and told Mandi about it.

I sat down and started writing page after page about my life. A week later, I had a dream in which one of my classmates from YWAM spoke to me. When I woke up, I didn't think anything of it until I opened my phone and saw a message from the same classmate. I contacted her and we started catching up. During our conversation, she told me about the YWAM School of Writing in Hawaii. As it turns out, she was planning to attend the writing school. After we talked, I thought about applying to the writing school because I had decided to start writing a book. I thought that maybe my dream and the conversation about writing with my classmate wasn't a coincidence. So, I applied to the writing school and was accepted a month later. But, though I was excited about being accepted, I didn't have all the money to go. I approached a few churches and, thankfully, they allowed me to hand out the letters and raise the funds through them.

By this time, Mandi had come to visit me once more and we were talking a lot. I was still working and was getting stressed about writing school coming up because I didn't know if it was really possible. I wondered if the support would come in. I prayed and tried to trust that, if it was God's will for me to go, it would work out. One day, I asked if God would give me a sign if I was to go to the writing school in Hawaii, and, a week later while at work, I started seeing people wearing Hawaiian t-shirts. I saw a pattern and finally caught on that it was God, though I didn't fully believe it until that night when I ran into one more person with a Hawaiian shirt. I started to laugh and understood it was the sign for which I had prayed. I felt encouraged that God was going to get me to the writing school in September.

A month before school, in August of 2019, Mandi and I were planning to meet in Lakeside, Montana, to see each other. About two weeks before we were to meet, I started thinking about proposing to Mandi. I prayed about it and decided I was going to ask her to marry me in Montana where we first met. I planned it out in my head, but I still needed a ring. I had visited the jewellery store a few times, but couldn't decide on a ring. I also knew I wasn't going to buy a ring until I had her father's blessing.

Mandi was travelling to Montana a week earlier than me, so I waited until she was there before I called her dad. It was a Wednesday night, and I was thankful to discover that he was happy to give me his blessing. The crunch was on! Since I was leaving the next Friday morning to drive to Montana, I had only one day to find a ring. After work on Thursday night, I went back to the same jewellery store and sat down beside a couple, who were also looking at rings. I was having trouble deciding on which ring to choose when the woman from the couple beside me asked if I wanted some help. I said "Yes, please!" She tried on rings for me so that I could see how they looked on a woman's hand.

While she was helping me, we started chatting about life. It turned out that we knew some of the same people and that they had just acquired some property in my hometown! We talked a lot about our lives, and I eventually found a ring that I liked. I thanked them as they got up to leave the store. But, even though I had found a ring, I was wrestling with whether or not I should spend such a large amount of money at this moment, since I was going to school in a month. As much as I was ready to propose,

I just wasn't sure I could afford buying the ring. So, I sat and prayed about it for a few moments. As soon as I finished praying, the woman who had tried on the rings for me came back into the store and sat down beside me. She offered to give me several hundred dollars towards buying the ring. I immediately started to cry because I was so overwhelmed by her generosity and kindness. I looked up as I accepted the gift and noticed that others were tearing up as well. It was a magical moment that I'll never forget, and I was able to walk out of the store with a ring.

I was filled with anticipation during the eight-hour drive to Lakeside, Montana. When I arrived, Mandi met me with hugs and smiles. It was great to see her in person. That evening, we went out for supper and had a wonderful time visiting. Somehow, I remained calm and collected, hoping the evening would go as planned. We showed up at Whitefish Lake, where we had had our first date, and I took her to the beach, where we were going to watch the sunset from "our bench." However, when we arrived, the beach was full. I thought my plan was spoiled because I had wanted to ask her there while we were alone. So, we went for a walk down the beach, and miraculously, when we returned, we watched in awe as the whole beach emptied and we were alone. We sat at "our bench" and watched the sun set over the lake.

As we sat there, I was so nervous, hoping to propose at some point. Finally, I mustered up the courage. I began by telling her that I had missed her while she was away and that I loved her. It was the first time we had said that to one another. At the same time, I pulled the ring out of my backpack and knelt down in front of her. I opened the little box with the ring and asked her to be my wife. She was so shocked that she just looked at me like a deer in the headlights and fell forward into my chest. I wasn't sure if she had responded or not, so I asked if she had said yes. She blurted out "yes!" twice in a row, and we hugged each other. I put the ring on her finger, and it fit perfectly. We took each other's hands and prayed, thanking Jesus for this moment. Over the next week of our time in Montana, we celebrated the news of our engagement with our special friends from the Crossroads Discipleship Training School.

WRITING SCHOOL

CHAPTER ELEVEN

I returned to Swift Current and worked my last month before leaving for Hawaii and the writing school. I was so humbled by the support I received through encouragement and financial blessings. I was so thankful, as God had provided exactly what I needed to attend the writing school. Everything was falling into place, and I was so excited.

Four weeks into the writing school, I started feeling pretty down. I wasn't a natural-born writer and I hadn't spent significant amounts of time writing, so I didn't understand why God would lead me to complete a writing school. I felt out of place among my classmates who seemed like stronger writers. I didn't believe that I was cut out for this writing school. Doubts filled my mind and I cried out to the Lord about it. One evening after class, I went for a walk downtown to the oceanfront. I remember stopping at one point and praying for help to continue with the writing school. I asked God, "Why am I here in Hawaii doing a writing school? I'm not a writer. Why me? Why am I here?"

I continued on my way. As I was walking, I came across two women: one who I had met earlier that week and one who wasn't familiar to me. So, I stopped and talked with them. Soon, the subject of counselling came up. I told them I had done some counselling because of the mental illness and hardships that had happened in my past. I shared that I had been diagnosed with Bipolar disorder at the age of twenty-two. They both gave me a weird look and then each of them confessed that they had been diagnosed with Bipolar as well.

I knew it wasn't a coincidence that I had just met two people who had the same mental illness as me. I returned to campus and saw that I received a Facebook message from an old friend. As we messaged back and forth, he started to tell me about his father, who was also wrestling with Bipolar. After being shocked again at God's timing, I gave him some advice on how to relate to and help his dad. As I sat humbled by what I had experienced in the last few hours, I began to cry, because God answered my prayer. In one night, He showed me the purpose for attending this writing school. I was to continue in it and write my story about living with mental illness.

I graduated from school four months later and was accepted to stay at the campus and complete an internship. Over the course of those months, as I shared with people why I was writing a book, many opened up with me about their friends and family who were struggling with Bipolar.

COVID-19

CHAPTER TWELVE

The spring of 2020 hit hard and fast, with the news of a pandemic sweeping the world. I was two weeks away from flying home from Hawaii. Flights were being cancelled fast, so I re-booked my flight and came home a week early. My plans changed a lot due to the COVID-19 outbreak. Mandi and I were slated to be married in July of 2020, but our long-distance relationship period just got longer. We weren't sure if the wedding could even take place, since the border between Canada and the U.S. was closed. With me living in Canada and Mandi living in the U.S., things were even more difficult.

A month before our wedding date, I found out that some people were still able to fly across the border, so I booked a flight to Pennsylvania. Then, two weeks before the wedding, social gatherings in Pennsylvania opened up from twenty-five to 250 people. We were able to go ahead with the wedding, even though no one from Canada was able to come. It was a beautiful wedding—probably the nicest one I've ever attended. All of our plans and details fell into place, and, on July 11, 2020, we were married. We broadcast it online for all to see. After the wedding, we went on a short honeymoon, as we had to get back to Canada to quarantine for two weeks before I returned to work. On our way back to Canada, we caught wind that the social gatherings had just decreased again—back down to twenty-five people. Praise the Lord for opening the window for us to be married in the midst of a pandemic! And, we didn't hear of one person getting sick at our wedding of 130+ people.

The last four years have been a whirlwind of blessings from God. First, was the five-month Discipleship Training School in Montana, where I met my wife. Next, I attended the YWAM writing school in Hawaii, and then I got married in July of 2020. Not quite ten months after our wedding, we celebrated the birth of our beautiful baby boy, Boaz, and, in the fall of 2022, we welcomed a baby girl named Tirzah.

EPILOGUE

Well there it is, forty-two years of life so far. I wonder if, in another twenty years, I'll write another book... maybe part two? I feel life is really starting to make sense, and I'm excited to see what God has in store for the rest of my days. I know now that God has a purpose and a plan for my life.

The stigma around mental health is changing, but I feel we need more people on the ground being vulnerable and sharing their stories. It's one thing to go on social media and share, but I believe it's also important to have in-person relationships and face-to-face communication. This allows us to be available to and connect one-on-one with people who are struggling. I believe vulnerability creates more vulnerability and allows others to have the strength to humble themselves so they can get the help they need.

If we need to look to someone about being humble, we need to look to the man of Jesus Christ, our loving Savior. Jesus humbled himself to the point of being crucified on a cross for our sins.

I know life isn't always easy—we were not promised that. But I also know that out of suffering and pain comes inextinguishable joy. When you go through tough times, you learn to persevere and see how God carried you through. I have learned to be thankful in good times and bad, because I know now Jesus is with me and will not ever leave me. I'm never alone.

Mental illness, suicide, and addictions are on the rise. The more we are isolated by social media and corrupt governments, the more these things are going to keep rising. I believe if you continue to follow the ways of the world, things are going to really hurt you and your family. The answer to our problems, and my success over those issues, is Jesus. Let's get back to the Bible and let God back into our lives. I know the devil is already defeated, but he is still out there, trying to destroy our lives. We have to stand firm in Christ for our protection.

I currently work in ministry with Rock Solid Refuge. I still feel passionate about the work that goes on there because I've seen many lives changed, from the teens and their families to the lives of the staff. The most change I've seen is when a student puts their faith in Jesus. I believe though that all who come through Rock Solid Refuge are changed in some way because they hear the Gospel and see it lived out.

I'm thankful for my wife. She is a rock, a Proverbs 31 woman. We are newly married and have two children together now. I feel life has been put in fast forward and the Lord has me on a path of blessing and leaving a lasting legacy.

My parents are doing well and I love them dearly. I'm thankful for the sacrifices they made for me—especially my mom. She has walked through some hard times with me and my mental health. God has blessed me with some incredible friends who have walked with me as well. There are so many people I am thankful to have in my life.

Shaunavon, SK volunteer fireman 10/09.

My eight second ride at the Businessman's
Bull Riding Event at Shaunavon Rodeo.

The look of a man that has been given new life in Christ.

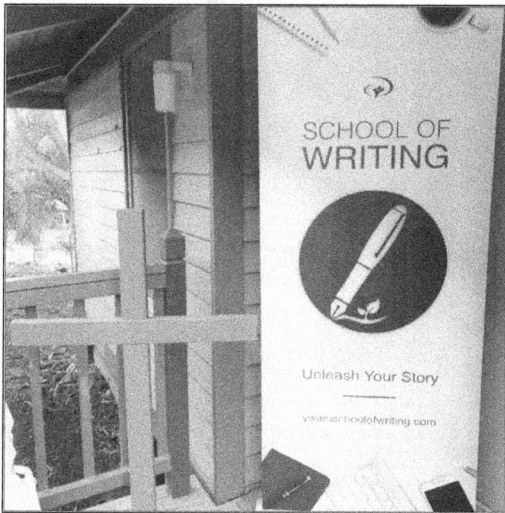

Six months spent in Hawaii doing a YWAM writing school in 2019/20.

My pregnant wife, Mandi, carrying our daughter,
Tirzah, and myself holding our son, Boaz (2022).

Starting DTS with YWAM in 2018 in Lakeside, Montana.

Wedding day July 11, 2020, in Pennsylvania.

My sister and I when we were little.

Smiling young Todd Bymoen.

Head wrangler at West Bank Bible Camp about ten years ago.

www.ingramcontent.com/pod-product-compliance
Lightning Source LLC
Chambersburg PA
CBHW071457070426
42452CB00040B/1556